The

Self-Publishing

Journal

Also Written By

Assuanta "Collins" Howard

Until the Next time
Until the Next Time 2: God's Plan

Collaborations

Assuanta Fay Howard & Marc Lacy
Wretched Saints:
When the Righteous Path Leads to Hell's Doorsteps

THE

SELF-PUBLISHING

JOURNAL

Assuanta Fay Howard

ASTA
PUBLICATIONS ™

ASTA
PUBLICATIONS ™

www.astapublications.com

Copyright © 2010 by Assuanta Fay Howard

Library of Congress Cataloging-in-Publication Data
    Howard Fay, Assuanta, The Self-Publishing Journal

p. cm
Includes index.

ISBN13: 978-1-934947-14-2
LCCN: 2009941188

Editors: Thelma C. Howard and Kim N. Carswell
Contributors: Kim N. Carswell and Kerry E. Wagner
Text and Composition: Asta Publications

Printed in the United States of America

Dedication

This book is dedicated to those who were told that they couldn't...

As my parents once told me there is so such word as can't.

Contents

Promoting Your Book 4

Selling Your Book 5

Your Self-Publishing To Do List 6

Suggested Reading...129

ABOUT THE AUTHOR

Assuanta Howard was born and raised in The Bronx, New York City. She is known for her dynamic and innovative persona. Her career began in higher education, serving over 17 years in various leadership roles. She managed grant funded programs with budgets over 3 million dollars. Howard is qualified to administer the Myers Briggs Type Indicator, a psychometric questionnaire designed to measure psychological preferences in how people perceive the world and make decisions. Howard took her extensive literacy and ESOL experience, leadership and program development expertise and established several business entities within the literary industry. She is the proud founder of Asta Publications, LLC, a mainstream and self-publishing company and Asta Public Relations Services, a public relations firm that focuses on brand management and marketing campaigns for literary professionals.

Howard holds a Master of Science degree in Adult Education and Human Resource Development from Fordham University and a Bachelor of Arts degree in Psychology and Early Childhood Education from the College of New Rochelle. She is also an active board member of the Fulton County Workforce Investment Board and serves as the chair of the Quality Assurance Taskforce. She also serves as the Chief Financial Officer for the National Independent Artist Networking Alliance Foundation (NIANAF).

In addition, she holds membership and affiliations with the following associations: American Counseling Association, the American Society for Training and Development, Independent Book Publishers Association, National Employment Counseling Association, Phi Kappa Phi Honor Society, the nation's oldest, largest, and most selective all-discipline honor society, Public Relations Society of America, The New York Center for Independent Publishing, and the Small Publishers Association of North America.

Assuanta Howard currently resides in Atlanta, Georgia.

ACKNOWLEDGMENTS

The Self-Publishing Journal is a result of my experience in the publishing industry. The knowledge gained over the years in due in part to the various people that have taken the time to share resources, information, and to encourage me to remain in this industry.

I would like to first acknowledge Erin Newhouse for showing me how to typeset a book professionally using Indesign. Erin is there whenever I need to call on her, and with this I am grateful.

Even though, we have only known each other for only one year, I must thank Kerry E. Wagner for pushing me when I didn't want to be or felt I couldn't do it any longer. This man is a master of knowledge beyond belief... don't sleep on him.

I want to thank Ms. Heisman, Blanche Kellowan, Dr. Jane MacKillop, and Deborah Douglass for always believing and supporting me. You ladies were the beginning of what I was to become. You knew what I was capable of... before I knew it.

And lastly, I want to thank my family for being the rock in my foundation: Mom, Dad, Kim, Douglas, Aunt Ruby, Mary, Yolanda, Michaelle, and Taylor.

Getting Started ~ 1

Nearly everyone wants to write a book. Most people have the ability, some have the drive, but few have the organization.

--Dan Poynter

First Things First

"In 2008, nearly 480,000 books were published or distributed in the United States, up from close to 375,000 in 2007, according to the industry tracker Bowker. The company attributed a significant proportion of that rise to an increase in the number of print-on-demand books."
~Books in Print

Have you ever thought about writing a book? If your answer is yes, this is the book for you. Everyone has a story to tell and one way of making sure your history, your message, and creativity are shared with others is to write a book. Some of us write hoping to get signed to a traditional publishing company; some of us store our stories onto computers and do nothing with it; and some of us decide to self-publish. For those of us that have the desire to write a book and do nothing about it, you must ask yourself why not. What is stopping you from realizing your dream of seeing your creativity on the bookshelf or in the hands of a reader? There are many reasons you can give yourself for not following through on the plans you've promised to complete, such as the list indicates below:

"It is hard to get picked up by a traditional publisher."
"I heard you must have a literary agent."
"Self-publishing is too much work."
"You can't write."
"No one wants to read what you've written."
"There are so many companies out there; I don't want to

get scammed."

"I have limited resources."

All of the responses mentioned above are valid and reasonable, huh? Every day you wake up and go through life not fulfilling your life's purpose, takes away from you as an individual. Excuses and circumstances shouldn't deter you from finding a way to make it happen. No more excuses, *get busy living or get busy dying* as entrepreneur Kerry E. Wagner often says.

The purpose of *The Self-Publishing Journal* is to get you motivated into accomplishing your goals of writing, completing, and publishing your book. Keeping a journal has many advantages and benefits that will help with setting and completing goals. Whether you write a few lines or pages; journaling will afford you the opportunity to record, keep track of your thoughts, and remain focused. When committing to writing your thoughts, ideas, and stories or poems down, you have put them into a solid form. Below are some examples of the benefits of keeping a journal.

Goal Setting - Clearly defines your writing routine and will produce steps towards completing your publishing goals.

Organization - Journaling your goals and what you want to accomplish for the day, the month, the year, or a lifetime, is an excellent tool to help you get those things done. You can create a personal checklist of "things to do."

Focus - Writing in a journal creates more personal awareness, and therefore more focus on the issues that are important to you. The routine habit of journaling means that you will be making time for you. When you set time aside for yourself, you will immediately feel the benefits that come with doing something specifically for yourself. It will show up in other areas of your life as you carry that time you have spent on yourself within you, and every-where you go.

The Self-Publishing Journal will help to keep you occupied with writing. With journal writing, you will practice writing something for a particular period of time; that is simple to practice, and something that will help you to become more active in other forms of writing. Lastly, journal writing is another good prevention against writer's block and boredom.

Writing is just the beginning of your journey and not the end.
~ Assuanta Howard

The Publishing Process

Self-publishing can be a wonderful solution for getting into print and puts you in control over your product. Publishing is a business and it is important that you research this new business venture. If your desire is to see your words in print and self-publishing is the route you've selected, then it would be in your best interest to do your homework. There are a lot of resources available, but you must seek it!

Let's define publishing and the various routes of getting your book to the masses.

Publishing

Publishing is the process of producing and disseminating literature or information for public view.

Commercial or Traditional Publishing

A commercial publisher distributes books under its' own imprint. It purchases manuscripts from authors, and handles the cost of producing those manuscripts: Cover and interior design, typesetting, printing, marketing, distribution, etc. The author is not expected to pay any of these costs. The books are owned by the publisher and remain in the publisher's possession until sold and the author receives a portion of sales in the form of royalties.

Vanity or Subsidized Publishing

Vanity or Subsidized publishing is often called Print-on-demand publishing, which is incorrect. Print-on-demand is a technology used to print books on demand. Vanity or Subsidized publishing provides publishing services to assist authors with getting their books to the market for a fee. Depending on the services needed; the costs range from $500 to $10,000. The services include but not limited to providing: ISBN, barcode, distribution, marketing, editing, printing, cover design, and more. There are many Vanity or Subsidized publishers that provide print-on-demand technology, which is beneficial to authors that do not have the resources to print a truck load of books and/or store them. One example of a publishing company that provides subsidized publishing along with print-on-demand technology is Asta Publications.

Self-Publishing

A self-publisher is an author who establishes a publishing business and is responsible for paying the cost of designing, printing, distributing, marketing, warehousing, and fulfillment.

As a self-publisher you must purchase an ISBN number. This number identifies the publisher. Note, if you decide to use a subsidized publisher's ISBN you will not be recognized as a self-publisher. This does not mean that they own the rights to your book, however they are listed as the publisher of the book. Some companies will allow you to use your own ISBN.

The cost to self-publish ranges from three thousand dollars to ten thousand dollars. This cost factors includes all phases of self-publishing to include: pre-production (editing, cover design, and interior design), production (printing), and post-production (proofreading, marketing, and distribution) costs.

Self-published books are the property of the author and all sales proceeds belong to the author. With the advancement of digital technology, books can be printed on demand; allowing you the freedom of ordering books as needed. Self-publisher can seek out subsidized publishing companies that provide stand-alone services such as: editing, cover design, typesetting, marketing, and distribution.

Now that you know the various modes to publishing, which one is right for you?

List the ten reasons you want to publish a book.

_____

_____

_____

_____

_____

Have you thought about submitting your manuscript to a traditional or commercial publisher? If yes, list five publishers you would like to consider your manuscript.

_____

_____

_____

_____

_____

Do you want to self-publish? Why or Why not. List your reasons below:

_____

_____

_____

_____

_____

_____

Do you have the finances to publish? If not, list five ways you can set aside money to fund your self-publishing venture.

_____

_____

_____

_____

_____

Do you have a completed manuscript? If yes, when do you plan to have it ready for publication? If no, when do you plan on completing your manuscript? For this exercise jot down a few tentative dates of completion or publication. These benchmark dates may change and that is okay.

_____

_____

_____

_____

I will act now. I will act now. I will act now. Henceforth, I will repeat these words each hour, each day, everyday, until the words become as much a habit as my breathing, and the action which follows becomes as instinctive as the blinking of my eyelids.

~ Og Mandino

Writing Your Book

So you've decided to write a book? Writing a book is not for the faint at heart. It takes a dedication and a lot of hard work. Due to busy schedules, at times you may feel as if time cannot be devoted to your writing, but if it is one of your goals, you must find the time to do it.

Saying you want to write a book is not enough! Once you've made the decision to write, stick to it. No excuses allowed.

Let's get started with your writing process:

Write down five reasons you want to write a book.

_____

_____

_____

_____

_____

Write down your daily schedule and how you will fit writing into it.

_____

_____

_____

_____

_____

Who are you writing for? Who will buy your book? Describe your reader. List characteristics, age, where they live, the types of books they like to read, etc.

_____

_____

_____

_____

_____

_____

_____

_____

Write down six things you are passionate about doing.

_____

_____

_____

_____

_____

_____

Of the six things you are passionate about write down three things you feel you would like to write about.

_____

_____

_____

_____

_____

_____

_____

_____

_____

Are you an expert in a particular subject? Think about your work experiences and educational background. List four areas you are very knowledgeable about.

_____

_____

_____

_____

_____

Determine the genre you would to write in. Think about the genres you like to read and write them down. Place a check mark next to the genres you think you would be good at writing.

☐ **Action**

☐ **Adventure**

☐ **Children**

☐ **Comedy**

☐ **Crime**

☐ **Drama**

☐ **Fantasy**

☐ **Historical/Epic**

☐ **Horror**

☐ **Inspirational**

☐ **Mystery**

- ☐ **Suspense/Thrillers**
- ☐ **Romance**
- ☐ **Science Fiction**
- ☐ **Urban**
- ☐ **Memoir**

Have you lived through a unique experience or associated with a celebrity? If so you might be able to write a memoir or autobiography. Write down five things about your life or someone you know that people might be interested in.

_____

_____

_____

_____

_____

_____

_____

_____

_____

Do you feel compelled to capture expressive messages for the fun of it? Are you a poet? Write a few lines from a poem you've written or in the process of writing.

_____

_____

_____

_____

_____

_____

_____

_____

_____

_____

You don't choose your story, it will choose you.
~ Assuanta Howard

SELECTING A TITLE

Selecting a title for a book can be a difficult process for some people. A good book title will greatly increase the marketability of your book. For the most part, readers will not read your entire book before purchasing it, so you want to grab them with your title and book cover. Naming your book is as personal as writing the book and is entirely up to you! Spend some time brainstorming ideas for a captivating title.

Write one paragraph describing what your book is about.

_____

_____

_____

_____

_____

_____

Read your paragraph and write down ten possible titles.
Your title should be catchy and descriptive.

_____

_____

_____

_____

_____

_____

_____

_____

_____

_____

_____

_____

_____

_____

Go to Amazon.com and put the ten titles in the search bar and see if your titles come up. You might get some ideas for additional titles. Write down five more titles.

_____

_____

_____

_____

_____

_____

_____

_____

_____

_____

_____

_____

Sum up your book in one sentence. Write a minimum of five one-liners. Remember, you have one chance to get your message out to others.

_____

_____

_____

_____

_____

_____

_____

A Few Tips on Selecting a Book Title:

- Keep it short
- Don't rely on the subtitle to explain the book.
- Avoid clichés
- Share your titles with others and get their opinions
- Use Descriptive words
- Be different and unique
- Research the title on Amazon or Google. Even though you can't copyright a title, you don't want to use a title that has been used too many times or belongs to a popular book.

Dr. Amos N. Wilson, (1941 - 1995) former Social Caseworker, Psychological Counselor, Supervising Probation Officer, Training Administrator in the New York City Department of Juvenile Justice, Assistant Professor of Psychology at the City University of New York, Master Teacher, Organizer, and Author.

Dr. Wilson was my professor when I was an undergrad at the College of New Rochelle in New York. I shared my desire to write a book with him and he encouraged me to do it. At the time, I was having a difficult time coming up with a title and his response will remain with me, forever, 'Don't stress over the title. Keep on writing, the title will come to you.' That was over fifteen years ago. When I wrote my first novel, "Until the Next Time", that is exactly what happened. The title didn't come to me until I was almost finished with the manuscript. The point I am making is that even after you've jotted down a few titles, your title may not come to you, but don't give up; keep on writing. No excuses, the title will come to you.

"Don't stress over the title. Keep on writing, the title will come to you."

~ Dr. Amos Wilson

Simple Self-Editing Techniques

Self-editing is the process of reviewing your own work. First things first; write the first draft of your manuscript without editing. You want to get all of your ideas on paper. It is recommended that after you've completed your manuscript to take a break prior to beginning the editing process. As you edit, be aware of your pet problems, such as omitting words, repeating certain words and phrases, or frequently misspelled words, punctuation and grammatical errors.

The first stage of edits should be substantive, where you look for issues regarding the overall flow of your manuscript. The second stage of edits is called a line edit. Review your manuscript line by line, sentence by sentence. Check for run-on sentences, sentences that are wordy, and ensure that your sentences are conveying the intended meaning. The third stage of edits are called copyedits. Run spell and grammar check on your computer and correct usage issues that come up. The last stage of the editing process is called proofreading. Proofreading is conducted after your manuscript has been typeset.

It is always helpful to get your work professionally edited. You can use these simple self-editing techniques to eliminate many of the grammar and stylistic issues that weaken your writing.

Pull your manuscript up and run a spell and grammar check on your computer.

Read your manuscript thoroughly. Is it clear? Jot down a minimum of ten things that makes your manuscript unclear.

_____

_____

_____

_____

_____

_____

_____

_____

_____

_____

_____

_____

Check for typos and misspelled words. Write down the typos and misspelled words you find in your manuscript. You might notice a pattern. As you go through another reread, use the list compiled to assist you with catching as many pet problems as possible.

_____

_____

_____

_____

_____

_____

_____

_____

_____

_____

_____

_____

_____

_____

_____

Are you using several words and phrases? Don't use the same words over and over again. Check your manuscript and list the words that have been repeated several times throughout the text.

_____

_____

_____

_____

_____

_____

_____

_____

_____

_____

_____

_____

_____

_____

_____

_____

_____

_____

_____

_____

_____

_____

_____

_____

_____

_____

_____

_____

_____

_____

Check your manuscript for tenses. Make sure you are not jumping from past tense to present tense when relating to events that take place within the same timeframe. Are you writing in first, second or third person? List the instances where you have jumped from past to present tense.

_____

_____

_____

_____

_____

_____

_____

_____

_____

_____

_____

_____

Check your manuscript for redundancy. Jot down the instances where you have mentioned a particular time period, introduced a character, mentioned a location, etc. Make sure to include the chapter and page number, so you can easily make changes.

_____

_____

_____

_____

_____

_____

_____

_____

_____

_____

_____

_____

Reminder verbs and subjects agree in number for example. That is, "she was" is correct; "they were" is correct. "They was" is incorrect. Review your manuscript line by line and write down the incorrect subject and verb agreements.

_____

_____

_____

_____

_____

_____

_____

_____

_____

_____

_____

_____

Here are some simple self-editing techniques to help you throughout the editing process:

- After you've completed your manuscript, put it down. Let some time lapse before attempting to edit it.

- Read the entire document first. Look at the content, organization, and flow. Make sure you've said all you want to say. Check to see if your manuscript makes sense. Add or delete phrases, words, sentences. Move things around and include transitions.

- Give yourself a week before doing a second read. On the second re-read, run spell and grammar check, correct any grammar, spelling, and punctuation errors as you come across them. Don't overdue it.

- Give yourself at least three days before doing a third read. On the third re-read look at your word choices. Could you have chosen another way to make your point? Do you need to revise sentences or paragraphs to make it clearer or more interesting?

- As you finish the last stage of editing, you are ready to have your book typeset. Typesetting is the process of laying out the interior pages of your book.

- You are ready for the proofreading stage after your manuscript has been typeset. Proofread for grammar, usage, spelling and punctuation. Read your manuscript aloud.

A bad book is as much of a labour to write as a good one; it comes as sincerely from the author's soul.
~ Aldous Huxley

Becoming an Authorpreneur ~2

Avoiding the phrase "I don't have time…," will soon help you to realize that you do have the time needed for just about anything you choose to accomplish in life.
~ Bo Bennett "Year to Success

Choosing a Name for Your Company

Publishing is a business. Choosing a name for your publishing business is an integral part of establishing your company. The first impression potential readers will have of your business may be based on its name. For this reason, the corporate name chosen matters, select a memorable name that will catch your reader's attention. Choosing a name for your company is similar to selecting a title for your book, you want to brainstorm different names to assist you with coming up with the right one for your business.

To jumpstart the process of creating names, ask yourself the following questions and write down the answers.

Are you planning to publish other authors in the future? Who is your intended audience? What genres are you planning to publish? Write your responses below:

_____

_____

_____

_____

Write down five phrases that might appeal to your readership?

_____

_____

_____

_____

_____

_____

_____

_____

Write down three words that appeal to you, based on your personality, likes, and dislikes.

_____

_____

_____

_____

Using the three words written above create three more new words. Use the thesaurus to find similar words to the one's written.

_____

_____

_____

_____

_____

_____

Other names to consider would be a nickname, surname, or family member names. List a few names below.

_____

_____

_____

_____

_____

_____

Things to consider:

- Say your remaining names aloud.
- Does the business name sound as good as it looks?
- Do you feel comfortable saying the name when someone calls you?
- Can a caller understand the name when you answer the phone?
- Would they be able to spell it easily?

Writing is the only thing that, when I do it, I don't feel I should be doing something else.

~ Gloria Steinem

Selecting Your Company's Structure

Starting a company is not difficult, but it takes hard work and dedication. Owning a business affords you the opportunity to deduct some of your expenses; such as the purchasing of a computer, paper, printing expenses, magazine subscriptions, mileage, airplane tickets, hotel fees, conferences, web site design, etc.

One of the first decisions that you will have to make as a business owner is how the company should be structured. This decision will have long-term implications, so consult with an accountant and attorney to help you select the form of ownership that is right for you.

There are different structures to choose from to include and for the purposes of this journal we will define the following: sole proprietorship, partnership, corporation, and limited liability company.

Sole Proprietorship

The sole proprietorship is a simple, informal structure that is inexpensive to form. It is usually owned by a single person or a marital community. The owner operates the business, is personally liable for all business debts, and can report profit or loss on personal income tax returns.

Advantages

- You are your own boss
- Less government regulation than other forms
- Simple structure
- Ease of formation
- Business losses lower personal tax

Disadvantages

- Risk losing business with death or disability
- Total personal liability
- Profits taxed as personal income
- Limited financial resources
- Limited management potential can only expand with "after tax dollars"

Partnership

Partnerships are inexpensive to form. They require an agreement between two or more individuals or entities to jointly own and operate a business. Profit, loss, and managerial duties are shared among the partners, and each partner is personally liable for partnership debts. Partnerships do not pay taxes, but must file an informational return. Individual partners report their share of profits and losses on their personal returns.

Advantages

- Simple organization

- Shared personal resources

- Shared financial resources

- The right to select partners

Disadvantages

- Cost of organization

- Unlimited liability

- Limited decision-making

- Limited life of business

- Sharing of profit

Corporation (Inc. or Ltd.)

This is a complex business structure with more startup costs than many other forms. A corporation is a legal entity separate from its owners, who own shares of stock in the company. Corporations may be subject to increased licensing fees and government regulation than other structures. Profits are taxed both at the corporate level and again when distributed to shareholders.

Shareholders are not personally liable for corporate obligations unless corporate formalities have not been observed; such formalities provide evidence that the corporation is a separate legal entity from its shareholders.

Failure to do so may open the shareholders to liability of the corporation's debts. Corporate formalities include: issuing stock certificates, holding annual meetings, recording minutes at the meetings, and electing directors or ratifying the status of existing directors. Seek a qualified attorney to assist with corporations.

Advantages

- Shared personal resources

- Shared financial resources

- Perpetual life increased management capability

- Easy transfer of business

- Limited personal liability

Disadvantages

- Possibility of double taxation

- Complex organization

- More costly operations

- More complicated management

- More government

Limited Liability Company (LLC)

The LLC is considered advantageous for small businesses because it combines the limited personal liability feature of a corporation with the tax advantages of a partnership and sole proprietorship. Profits and losses can be passed through the company to its members or the LLC can elect to be taxed like a corporation. LLC's do not have stock and are not required to observe corporate formalities. Owners are called members, and the LLC is managed by these members or by appointed managers.

In making a choice, ask yourself the following:

What is the vision or nature of your company?

_____

_____

_____

_____

_____

_____

_____

_____

_____

_____

How much personal control do you want to maintain over business decisions?

_____

_____

_____

_____

_____

_____

What will happen to the business if you are no longer able to manage it?

_____

_____

_____

_____

_____

_____

Evaluate the forms of business structures provided in the book and write down the advantages and disadvantages of each as it relates to your needs.

_____

_____

_____

_____

_____

_____

_____

_____

_____

_____

_____

_____

_____

_____

_____

_____

_____

_____

_____

_____

_____

_____

Vision is not enough, it must be combined with venture. It is not enough to stare up the steps, we must step up the stairs.

~ Vaclav Havel

CREATING YOUR BUDGET

Planning is an integral part of your publishing business. One of the things you want to do is devise a budget for your book projects. A budget is a plan for managing your money. It is an estimate of income and expenses over a period of time.

The first step to create a budget is to determine how much money you've spent on creating your book. This is called your expenses. Expenses are anything you spend money on book production. You will need to write down every dollar spent on creating your book.

To help you keep track of your initial expenses, write down the cost of each below:

Title of Book

Expenses			
Business License			
Copyright			
ISBN			
Editing			
Cover Design			
Interior Layout			
Printing			
Distribution			
Publishing Services Provider			

Selecting the price for your book

Printing is not the only factor to consider when setting the retail price. As a self-published author you must be concerned about your margin and your profit. Readers are not concerned with what you paid for the book nor are the retailers. Everyone wants a competitive price.

With over 400,000 books published each year in the U. S. alone, it is important to price your book in a range that is acceptable for your particular genre or category.

Go to Amazon.com or your local bookstore and pick at last five books that have similar trim sizes and page counts. Write down the titles and costs below:

_____

_____

_____

_____

_____

_____

_____

Take into account the "per unit" cost of your book. This cost is determined by the expenses incurred, such as editing, cover design, proofreading, interior layout, artwork, illustrations, cover design, and ISBN. Take a look at the above expense sheet and write down your costs. Take a look at the **Suggested Book Pricing Chart** on page 50 to see your profit margin.

_____

_____

_____

_____

_____

_____

_____

_____

_____

_____

_____

_____

Total Page Count	Paperback Cover Price	Hardback Cover Price
48-85	$7.95-$10.95	--
104-200	$11.95-14.95	$19.95-$25.95
204-300	$15.95- $17.95	$26.95-$28.95
304-400	$18.95-$20.95	$29.95-$31.95
500+	$21.95-$25.95	$31.95+

Discounts

Discounts are a necessary part of the book business. A large percentage of your sales to be through distributors, wholesalers, and bookstores -- and each of these will require a discount. Even direct consumers are likely to expect a discount for multiple-copy orders.

Distributor or Wholesaler discounts. Distributors like Ingram require a 55% discount, but your book will be available for purchase in major bookstores. Ingram requires that you have a minimum of ten titles before they consider you. Baker & Taylor is a wholesaler and is much easier to sign up with for an additional fee. They require a 55% discount. They cater to libraries and bookstores as well. However, a distributor can mean good business for you; if your book sells well, you may get orders for several hundred copies at a time.

Online bookstore discounts. Amazon.com's Advantage Program for small presses and self-published authors can be a helpful way to move your books online -- but it also means accepting a discount of at least 55%. Amazon will also charge you a fee of $29.95 to participate. Before you sign up for the program, keep in mind that books listed in *Books in Print* are listed in the online bookstores anyway. However, if your book must be special-ordered from the publisher (you), customers will be told that delivery may take several weeks, while the Advantage Program guarantees immediate delivery.

The man who can drive himself further once the effort gets painful is the man who will win.
~ Roger Bannister

Book Production ~ 3

Progress lies not in enhancing what is, but in advancing toward what will be.
--Kahlil Gibran

THE ART OF COVER DESIGN

Once your manuscript is completed and the final edits are done, you are ready to formalize it into a book. Cover Design in the self-publishing process may be considered the most intimate tenets of the book production process. It becomes the face of your thoughts and aspirations for the characters or themes in the manuscript.

Creating an eye catching cover is a combination of art, branding, skill, talent, preference, and most importantly your target audience. The book cover design process includes the front cover, back cover, barcode, ISBN, jacket (hardcover) and spine.

To jumpstart the process of visualizing your next book cover, ask yourself the following questions and write down the answers.

_____

_____

_____

_____

_____

When you visit your favorite bookstore or library: What types of books draw your attention? Are they in the same genre as your book? Write your responses below:

_____

_____

_____

_____

_____

_____

_____

_____

_____

_____

_____

_____

_____

_____

Write down the five images that come to mind when you think about your book? Do you have a favorite color(s) you would like to see with the images? Go to www. istockphoto.com or www.dreamtimes.com and select a stockphoto(s) that catch your attention. Write down the photo numbers below.

_____

_____

_____

_____

_____

_____

_____

_____

_____

_____

_____

_____

What type of font (typography) do you want to use? Times Roman and Arial are most commonly used fonts, but there are thousands available for use. Google fonts and take a look at the many different ones available. Again as you look at other books, pay attention to the size and placement of the text on the front cover, back cover, and the spine. Jot down the names of the fonts you like below. If you are designing your own cover, make sure to select fonts that are free of charge.

_____

_____

_____

_____

_____

_____

_____

_____

_____

_____

Do you plan to have your picture on the back? Will you solicit reviews before your book cover goes into print? If yes, write down the names of potential reviewers along with their contact information.

_____

_____

_____

_____

_____

_____

_____

_____

_____

_____

_____

_____

_____

WHAT IS TYPESETTING?

One of the major components to transferring your manuscript into a book is the composition, book layout or typesetting phase. This is when your words are placed in a format which is pleasant to the reader. The typesetting phase also marks the end of the editing process and the beginning of the interior design phase.

The first part of the phase is to determine what type of typography (fonts) you want to use and the size of your book. Again, one of the benefits of self-publishing is that the author dictates how they want their product to look and feel.

In addition, the typesetting process dictates the final page count. Most typesetters use professional software comparable to Adobe InDesign. Many self-published authors use Word to typeset their books. Keep in mind, that part of the printing costs are determined by the overall number of pages. Therefore the overall size of the book and page count will help you determine the suggested retail price.

When determining how your page layout will be, ask yourself the following questions and write down the answers.

When you open one of your favorite books, what do the headers look like? Is the authors name on the top of the page? If yes, which side of the book is it?

_____

_____

_____

_____

_____

Select three different books within your genre. Write down the title of each book and respond to the following questions. What does the Chapter pages include? How are the Chapter pages positioned? On the left, right or both? Are there numbers on each page? Are the numbers centered, flushed outside or next to the headers?

_____

_____

_____

_____

_____

_____

What type of font (typography) do you want to use for the interior? Does it compliment your book cover? Select at least five fonts you like. Next to the five fonts selected, decide where you would like the font placed in your book. (Headers, Chapter Headings, main story, etc.)

_____

_____

_____

_____

_____

_____

_____

_____

_____

_____

_____

_____

_____

THE PRINTING PROCESS

There are basically two main options for printing books: offset and digital. Offset printing offers excellent quality, but can be costly when ordering low quantities (less than 1,000). Offset printers also give you the option of using freight delivery or parcel post. Freight delivery has additional costs such as: delivery inside, the use of the lift gate, etc. Where as parcel post is UPS, FedEx or regular mail service. Digital printing offers quality close to offset and allows you to print smaller quantities. However, it is not a cost effective option when printing larger quantities. For example an offset print run of 10,000 copies of a 228 page book may cost you .65 cents per copy. Whereas the same print run using digital technology may cost you $1.08 per copy.

Advantages of offset printing

1. Higher image quality, higher resolution and no streaks/spots.
2. Works on a wide range of printing surfaces including paper, wood, cloth, metal, leather, rough paper and plastic.
3. The unit cost goes down as the quantity goes up.
4. Quality and cost-effectiveness in high volume jobs
5. Many modern offset presses use computer-to-plate (as opposed to the older computer-to-film system) further increasing quality.

Advantages of digital printing

1. Shorter turnaround
2. Lower costs for very small print runs
3. Availability of variable data printing (database driven, e.g. mailing lists)

Before selecting a printer, ask for samples and references.

How many books can you afford to print? Contact at least three printers from the Internet and get a quote for offset printing in quantities of 1,000, 3,000, and 5,000. Offset **printing** has a front-end cost load, which means short runs (low quantities) may have a high per-unit cost. But as quantities increase, the unit cost goes down with **offset printing.** Compare quotes below.

Contact at least three printers that provide digital printing from the Internet and get a quote for digital printing in quantities of 50, 100, and 500. Very short runs can be more cost effective with digital printing; while larger quantities are likely to have a lower unit cost with offset printing. Compare quotes below.

How soon do you need your books? Digital printing offers a quicker delivery. Some printers are offering 24 hour turnaround time. From the list of printers contacted, ask them their turnaround time and what make sure to compare the costs. Write their responses below.

_____

_____

_____

_____

_____

_____

_____

_____

_____

_____

_____

_____

Commitment leads to action. Action brings your dream closer.
~ Marcia Wieder

Promoting Your Book ~ 4

You have to expect things of yourself before you can do them.
--Michael Jordan

THE ABC'S OF BRANDING

Creating a brand is both a simple and challenging task. Brand development orchestrates ideas, images and concepts your colleagues, media outlets, and target audiences walk away with, when they hear your name and or see one of your book covers. Branding is a science of consistently living up to what you market. How many times have you bought something based on advertising, enticing words, and vivid pictures, later on to find it was not what you anticipated?

Branding is a guarantee, it is not hype surrounded by smoke and mirrors. It is the steady fulfillment of a promise to your potential readership. Personal branding involves the essence of who you are; your personality, credentials, and attire. The goal of literary branding is to capture the interior significance of authorship, building brand awareness, while aligning books (products) to an intended audience. Branding answers the old question; what makes a person buy one book over another?

Since you are now more familiar with the importance of branding, let's start outlining your brand by completing the excercises on the following pages.

Go to the library, bookstore, or your bookshelf and take a look at three of your favorite books. Identify the brand of each book/author. How do they position their brands? Write your observations below.

_____

_____

_____

_____

_____

_____

_____

_____

_____

_____

_____

_____

_____

When you think about your favorite author, what do they look like? Do they maintain a certain style? Write your observations below. Take a look at your own wardrobe; does your wardrobe match the author image you want to project? List your responses below.

_____

_____

_____

_____

_____

_____

_____

_____

_____

_____

_____

_____

_____

Does your message connect with your image and ultimately your target audience? Explain.

_____

_____

_____

_____

_____

_____

_____

_____

_____

_____

_____

_____

_____

_____

What colors represent your style or image? You want to choose colors that will be vibrant and can be used on your book cover, within your press kits, and on your web site. Write down your favorite colors below.

_____

_____

_____

_____

_____

_____

_____

_____

_____

_____

_____

_____

_____

What can your reader expect from you each time they read your book? Think carefully before responding, because this will be your brand promise. Jot down your responses below.

_____

_____

_____

_____

_____

_____

_____

_____

_____

_____

_____

_____

_____

Basic Media Kit

Packaging your message and your expertise is an essential piece to connecting with the media. A media kit also referred to as a "Press Kit" accentuates your brand. It answers the Who, What, When, Where, Why, and How for interested editors, writers, and reporters about your product and or business.

Media kits can be in both digital and print ready formats. If you decide to launch a web site, create a direct press or media kit link. You want to make it easier for the media to learn about you at a glance.

The media kit should include:

- Folder – Be creative with color and texture, but not with quality. Make sure it has at least one pocket.

- Business Card – Include a business card to serve as a quick contact reference.

- Contact/ Fact Sheet – Include your contact information and where your book can be found.

- Collateral Material – brochures postcards, flyers with logo or image of your book, and bookmarks.

- Author Biography – Compose one to two paragraphs about yourself to highlight and or supplement awards, recognition, expertise, and credentials.

- Head Shot – Make sure it is professional and it is at least 300 dpi (dots per inch) for digital reproduction and 72 dpi for web usage.

- Review Sheet – List the most compelling and substantive reviews that to complement your writing and expertise. You may use reviews from Amazon and Barnes and Noble.

- Articles- Include articles written about you. You may include articles written online as well.

- Press Releases – Past news features of both the author and their material. Press releases are a brief synopsis of literary and substantive events that would appeal to media outlets.

- Social Media Releases (SMR) – New complimentary public relations tool for the traditional press release. SMR's system engages readers with multimedia content throughout social networking sites and tracking sites such as Google News, Twitter, and Facebook.

Since we have outlined the ground rules which make up a standard media kit; ask yourself the following questions and write down the answers.

Visit ten author's web site and take a look at the photos in their media kits. Choose self-published and traditionally published authors. Rate each photo from a range of 1 to 5; with 5 being the best.

_____

_____

_____

_____

_____

What background information will you include in your Author Biography? List the following: Education, Work Experience, Accomplishments, etc.)

_____

_____

_____

_____

_____

_____

_____

_____

_____

_____

_____

_____

_____

Compile a list of people you would like to review your book.

_____

_____

_____

_____

_____

_____

_____

_____

_____

_____

_____

_____

_____

_____

_____

_____

_____

_____

Write down some things you have done in the past that would be newsworthy.

_____

_____

_____

_____

_____

_____

BENEFITS OF SOCIAL NETWORKING

In a nutshell social networking or social media marketing is a cost effective and efficient way to get your readers, media, and colleagues familiar with your history and engaged in your products. Some of the major networking sites are: Facebook, Twitter, and MySpace. Blogs are also useful tools to engage readers in your literary work.

Senator Barack Obama led a momentous presidential campaign which sparked a political movement. The Obama campaign was ushered in by the social networking industry, thus setting a new standard for how political campaigns should be run. In January 2008, I noticed the number (16) of social sites his campaign was affiliated with. Each site was representative of diverse segments of the United States and many had international appeal.

Unbeknownst to his opponents and many in the public, the co-founder of Facebook opted to step down from his post and join Barack Obama's campaign. Thus lending his expertise to designing the MyBO.org site which allowed supporters to meet and greet each other, host political house parties, register voters, schedule door-to-door campaign activities, and most of all generate the largest amount of political contributions to date. According to the Federal Elections Commission now President Barack Obama raised over 744 million dollars.

In addition, Microsoft also recognized the power of the social network and bought 1.6% of FaceBook's stock for $240 million dollars in October 2007. What does this tell authorpreneurs? Use your time and energy to get your brand on the social network highway. It gives you a cost effective method to make connections with your audience or at least media outlets that can expand your brand, image, and readership.

The wonders of social networking and social media marketing allow you the freedom to create accounts for both you as the author and individual sites for each book.

Are you a member of a social networking site? If yes, is it consistent with the image you want to express as an author? List the sites you are a member of.

_____

_____

_____

_____

_____

_____

Do you have photographs to upload onto the social networking site? Are you familiar with the process? Are you comfortable with posting pictures? If not why? Jot down your responses below.

_____

_____

_____

_____

_____

It is important to evaluate the success of your social networking efforts. Note you will spend a lot of time on these sites and it is extremely important that you maximize the time spent toward promoting your book. How do you plan to evaluate the success of your social media marketing efforts? List your responses below.

_____

_____

_____

_____

_____

_____

Research 5 social networking sites and write down the major differences between each:

_____

_____

_____

_____

_____

_____

_____

_____

_____

_____

_____

_____

_____

_____

Selling Your Book ~ 5

Real integrity is doing the right thing, knowing that nobody's going to know whether you did it or not.
--Oprah Winfrey

Targeting Your Audience

Publishing is a business. Your book is the product and your customers are readers. To successfully sell your book, you must identify who your readers are and determine how you will reach them.

Writing the book is just the start.

Think about the following questions for a moment:

Why should anyone purchase your book? Who is going to sell your book? How will anyone know you have written a book? Do you think everyone is a potential reader of your book?

You will need to answer the questions above and devise a marketing strategy to succeed. Remember you will be the number one promoter of your book and who better than you to reach your readers.

Identify your book's target audience. Does your book appeal more to females or males. Your response must include why or why not. Jot down your responses below.

_____

_____

_____

_____

_____

_____

Who is your ideal reader? (male or female, age range, educational level, interests) Provide key characteristics and specifics.

_____

_____

_____

_____

_____

_____

_____

_____

_____

_____

_____

_____

_____

What type of magazines do your readers subscribe to?
List them.

_____

_____

_____

_____

_____

_____

What movies do your readers watch? What blogs do they read? List them.

_____

_____

_____

_____

_____

Which radio station do they listen to? List them.

_____

_____

_____

_____

_____

_____

_____

_____

What makes your book a cut above your competition?
Write down ten things that makes your book competitive.

_____

_____

_____

_____

_____

_____

_____

_____

_____

_____

_____

_____

_____

_____

_____

_____

_____

List the web sites and blogs that would be frequented by your readers.

In your opinion, what is the most effective way to reach your audience?

_____

_____

_____

_____

_____

_____

_____

_____

_____

_____

_____

_____

_____

_____

_____

MARKETING & PROMOTIONS 101

Unless you've been on the Oprah Winfrey Show, you want to start off your marketing efforts locally. Capitalize on the area where you live, you can gradually expand your efforts after you've saturated your local market. Local media outlets such as radio, television, and newspapers will be more interested in featuring you.

As a new author it is important for you to connect with your readers by attending as many events as possible. Create a Myspace, Facebook, WordPress, Author Den, and Book Tour accounts. There are a lot of authors promoting their books and listing their events. You can contact those locations and schedule a book signing or participate in the event. Attending trade shows and book festivals are great ways to find readers... potential buyers. Wagfest International Networking Mixer mission is to cultivate an atmosphere for successful business practices in the entertainment and arts industries in a festive and inspiring way. This event is held in Atlanta on a yearly basis. The Book Expo of America is an industry event that happens annually and is another event to attend if you are interested in meeting people in the industry such as: other authors, librarians, editors, illustrators, foreign licensing people, suppliers, editors, etc.

Creating an online presence is crucial for online book sales. Creating a web site is the first part; you will also have to drive people to your web site. Your web site should contain content features that will interest people into buying your book. Blogs and Virtual Book tours are good ways to attract potential readers. Before you get started on building your web site, you are going to need a domain name and a host. Ipowerweb.com and GoDaddy.com are just two companies that provide this service. They also have templates you can use until you can afford to hire a web designer.

You must use all of your contacts to network, find creative publicity stories, angles and outlets, and generate ideas that'll get noticed and talked about.

Examples of Marketing:

1. **Fake publicity stunt**

2. **Guest blogging**- Guest blog on other blogs largely related, or semi-related to your web sites niche.

3. **Postcards/Bookmarks**- Go into the library and/ or bookstore and go to the section where your book will be placed and put your postcards and or bookmarks into every book. Karen Quino-nes Miller, author and literary agent suggested at a conference I attended, was to go to one of those newspaper bins that are usually outside of establishments and purchase one newspaper. While the box is open, place your postcard and/ or bookmark inside of the remaining newspapers.

4. **Sponsor an event**

5. **Charity donations-** You can donate some of your

clothing, coats, or proceeds from your book to a charity.

6. **Enter Contests**

It's your turn, list twenty out-of-the box things you can do to promote your book on a budget.

_____

_____

_____

_____

_____

_____

_____

_____

_____

_____

Getting Your Book into the Market

Distributors and Wholesalers

The differences between a distributor and a wholesale distributor (a.k.a. wholesaler) are subtle, but very important. Distributors employ a sales staff that calls book buyers for wholesalers, national chains, regional chains, and independent bookstores in a proactive effort to promote sales. A wholesaler operates on more of a reactive mode, like a warehouse or fulfillment site, making books available to purchase.

Distributor: Can get your book on the shelves at Costco, Borders, Barnes & Noble, etc. They take a percentage of your sales ranging from 55% to 65%. Many distributors will not deal with small publishers or self-published authors, unless you can place four or more of your titles with them at once or if you have a strong track record. There are distributors that work with self-published authors. Most distributors require an exclusive contract with them. This means you cannot place your book with another distributor.

Wholesaler: The percentage is 55%. Ingram is the top wholesaler and will only accept your application if you have more than ten titles. Your contract with a wholesaler is non-exclusive. Baker & Taylor is another wholesaler that works with self-published authors and small publishing companies.

Most distributors and wholesalers require that you submit a marketing plan along with a copy of your book for consideration. They do not accept titles that are printed or listed through print-on-demand or vanity publishers.

Any decent distributor and a few larger wholesalers will get your book listed on Ingram's list. In most cases if a book isn't listed with Ingram it doesn't exist, so when conducting your research, you want to make sure the distributor or wholesaler has an account with Ingram.

Research, research, and more research. Talk to different authors and find out who distributes their book. Contact different distributors and find out their success rates for placing books such as yours.

Compile a list of the pros and cons of signing an exclusive or non-exclusive contract.

_____

_____

_____

_____

_____

Google distributors and wholesalers. List their addresses, phone numbers and email addresses.

_____

_____

_____

_____

_____

_____

_____

_____

_____

_____

_____

_____

_____

_____

Now that you've compiled your list, the next step is to interview and evaluate the distributor or wholesaler, prior to making your final decision.

Ask each company representative the following questions and keep track of their responses.

Are they actively seeking new publishers to distribute?

_____

_____

_____

_____

_____

_____

_____

_____

_____

_____

It is important that the distributor you work with is familiar with your genre. Ask them what their most successful titles are and list them.

_____

_____

_____

_____

_____

_____

_____

_____

_____

_____

_____

_____

Find out if their contract is exclusive or non-exclusive. Write down their responses below.

_____

_____

_____

_____

_____

_____

_____

_____

_____

_____

_____

_____

_____

Find out how many publishers they work with. Get the names of the publishers. Contact some of these publishers to find out what their experience has been with the distributor.

_____

_____

_____

_____

_____

_____

_____

_____

_____

_____

_____

_____

Who are their primary customers: bookstores, public libraries, schools, universities, mass merchandisers, etc.?

_____

_____

_____

_____

_____

_____

_____

_____

_____

_____

_____

_____

Do they have any sales reps? If yes, how many and how often do they make sales calls? Ask them about the methods they use. (Cold calls, e-blasts, or if they have existing relationships with book buyers.)

_____

_____

_____

_____

_____

_____

_____

_____

_____

_____

_____

_____

Do they actively market and sell to major retailers such as Borders, Barnes and Noble, and Amazon? Which ones? How many titles do these stores purchase on a monthly basis?

What is the minimum discount they need from publisher-partners? You might be able to negotiate the rate.

_____

_____

_____

_____

_____

_____

_____

_____

_____

_____

_____

_____

_____

Find out the discounts they offer their library or bookstore customers. List their responses below.

_____

_____

_____

_____

_____

_____

_____

_____

_____

_____

_____

_____

_____

_____

_____

What are their requirements for establishing a distribution relationship (basic contract terms, marketing materials needed, and payment policies)? This is very important.

_____

_____

_____

_____

_____

_____

_____

_____

_____

_____

_____

_____

Do they have a catalog? How often is it updated? Is there an additional fee?

_____

_____

_____

_____

_____

_____

_____

What is their turnaround time between receiving an order and shipping the materials? Do they have any references to verify it? List their references.

_____

_____

_____

_____

_____

_____

_____

_____

_____

How often do they communicate with their publisher-partners?

_____

_____

_____

_____

_____

_____

_____

_____

_____

Even though distributors have a sales team, you are still responsible for marketing your book.

You want to make sure the distributor is representing, promoting, and selling your title to retailers.

What specific marketing efforts would be used to promote your titles? List them below.

_____

_____

_____

_____

_____

_____

_____

_____

_____

_____

_____

Find out if they attend trade shows throughout the year.
List the shows they attend and exhibit. Ask them if their
authors are allowed to sign at their booth.

_____

_____

_____

_____

_____

_____

_____

_____

_____

_____

_____

_____

_____

Other than catalogs and trade shows, do they engage in marketing or PR campaigns for individual publishers?

_____

_____

_____

_____

_____

_____

_____

_____

_____

_____

_____

_____

_____

Your Self-Publishing To Do List ~6

*To accomplish great things we must first dream, then
visualize, then plan... believe... act!*
-- Alfred A. Montapert

Self-publishing provides you with the opportunity to maintain control over your creative process. In order to become successful at publishing, it is important that you plan out your project carefully and set realistic goals.

I've included a simple "To Do List" to assist you with keeping track of the things you need to do to accomplish your self-publishing goals.

1. Determine your business structure, name your publishing company.
2. Check your State's guidelines for establishing a business. You will need to conduct a name search and apply for your business license.
3. Contact the IRS to get a Tax ID number.
4. Sign up for a post office box or a box at a mailbox store to use for business correspondence.
5. Open a business checking account.
6. Go to R. R. Bowker and order a block of International Standard Book Numbers (ISBN). You will assign one number to each book you publish. This number identifies your publishing company, the book, and is necessary for books sold in the retail market. For more information and to purchase your ISBN printout, visit www.isbn.org Contact the Agency by phone: 877-310-7333 or email: isbn-san@bowker.com.
7. Contact your State Board of Equalization and request a resale permit.

8. Assign an ISBN to your book.

9. Search for a printer. If you're going the traditional printing route, send a "Request for Price Quote" to eight or ten printers and ask to see samples of their work. The printer will want to know the quantity of books, number of pages, type of binding, paper stock, book dimensions, type of illustrations, text color, and cover ink (4-color)

10. Send pre-publication review copies.

11. Hire a cover designer.

12. Set your price.

13. Order a barcode. Contact Bar Code Graphics, Inc. at sales@barcode-us.com. You will need an ISBN and the price of the book in order for the company to create your barcode.

14. Select a printing method and a printer. United Graphics and Colorhouse Graphics are two printers I work with on a regular basis. Contact Steve Sirlin at United Graphics and Sandy Gould at Colorhouse Graphics.

15. Give the book to the printer

16. Solicit pre-publication orders.

17. Go online and complete the copyright registration. www.copyright.gov.

18. Start planning your promotion program.

19. Ship and deliver review copies, complimentary copies, and pre-publication orders.

20. Send a copy of your book to the Library of Congress.

21. Contact distributors and wholesalers.
22. Execute your promotional plan.

Resources
Suggested Reading

My great concern is not whether you have failed, but whether you are content with your failure.
--Abraham Lincoln

1. The Self-Publishing Manual: How to Write, Print and Sell Your Own Book by Dan Poynter
2. The Complete Guide to Self-Publishing: Everything you need to know, to write, publish, promote, and sell your own book by Tom & Marilyn Ross
3. How to Succeed in the Publishing Game by Vickie M. Stringer and Mia McPherson
4. The Self-Publishing Journal by Assuanta Fay Howard
5. Get Published by Susan Driscoll and Diane Gedymin
6. Publishing for Profit Successful Bottom-Line Management for Book Publishers by Thomas Woll
7. I'm Going to Tell You What They Don't Want You to Know by Kerry E. Wagner
8. The Copyright Permission and Libel Handbook A Step-By Step Guide for Writers, Editors, and Publishers by Jassin J. Lloyd and Steven Schechter

9. Classroom in a Book: Adobe InDesign CS4 by Adobe Systems or the most recent version
10. Bookmaking by Marshall Lee
11. The Chicago Manual of Style (Latest Edition)
12. Elements of Style by William Strunk Jr., E. B. White, and Roger Angell
13. The McGraw-Hill Handbook of English Grammar and Usage by Mark Lester and Larry Beason
14. The McGraw-Hill Desk Reference for Editors, Writers, and Proofreaders by K.D. Sullivan and Merilee Eggleston
15. Merriam Webster Dictionary and Thesaurus Newest Edition
16. 1001 Ways to Market Your Books for Authors and Publishers by John Kremer
17. The 22 Immutable Laws of Branding by Al Ries and Laura Ries

ASTA
PUBLICATIONS ™

To book Assuanta Howard to speak at your location, contact her at acollins@astapublications.com.

To learn more about Asta Publications and Asta Public Relations Services visit the following web sites: www.astapublications.com and www.astaprservices.com.

To join the National Independent Artist Networking Alliance Foundation, visit www.wagfestlitertainment.com.

For Branding information, visit www.personaaffairs.com